A Farm Visit

by William Overturf
illustrated by Meredith Johnson

Core Decodable 107

McGraw Hill Education
Bothell, WA • Chicago, IL • Columbus, OH • New York, NY

MHEonline.com

Send all inquiries to:
McGraw-Hill Education
8787 Orion Place
Columbus, OH 43240

ISBN: 978-0-02-138067-1
MHID: 0-02-138067-8

Printed in Canada.

9 10 11 12 KOD 24

Miss Dock drove the bus to a farm. The class looked out the windows. They saw meadows, barns, and silos.

Some of the meadows had wire fences. Some had low stone walls.

"Those stone walls have big rocks," said Joan.

The kids were from the city. Some had never seen a farm.

"Is that an ox?" asked Donnie.

Miss Dock smiled. "Nope, it looks a bit like an ox. But it is just a big cow."

"Ick! It is eating grass," said Joan.

Miss Dock slowed down the bus. "We eat grass, too," she said.

"No way!" said Joan.

The cow was mooing now.

Miss Dock drove the bus over a bumpy road.

"What did you eat for breakfast?" Miss Dock asked.

"A little box of Rice Puffs," Joan said.

"A bowl of oatmeal," said Donnie.

"You both had grass, then," said Miss Dock.

The bus was going slowly down the road. The road had big holes. Miss Dock had to dodge them.

"Rice is grass?" asked Joan.

"Oatmeal is not green," said Donnie. "How can oats be grass?"

Miss Dock parked the bus at the farmer's house. She looked at the farmer's lawn.

"I will show you," said Miss Dock.

Miss Dock and the kids got out of the bus. She picked a piece of very tall grass from the lawn.

"Look," said Miss Dock. "This blade of grass has little seeds on top."

Miss Dock dropped little seeds in her hand.

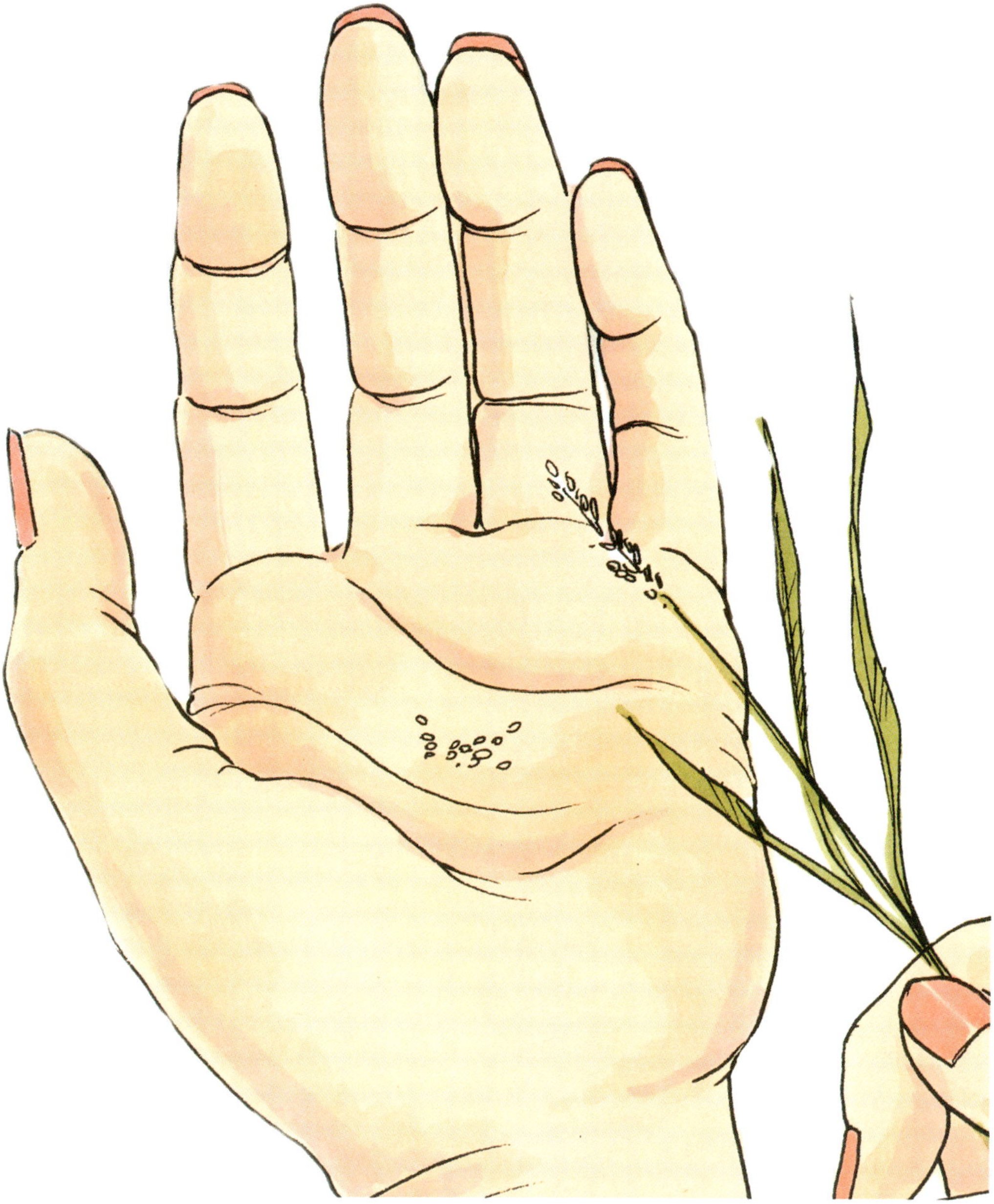

"Rice is a grass," said Miss Dock. "Seeds from it make food. And seeds from oat grass make food, too."

"Donnie, you know what that means," Joan said.

"Yes," smiled Donnie. "Moo!"

"Moo!" joined in Joan.